Bullying
IN SCHOOLS

What You Need to Know

Copyright © 2011 by Townsend Press, Inc.
Printed in the United States of America
ISBN-13: 978-1-59194-249-8
ISBN-10: 1-59194-249-7

Library of Congress Control Number: 2011928866

All rights reserved. No part of this work may be reproduced in any form
without permission in writing from the publisher. Send requests to
Townsend Press, Inc. at the address below.

Townsend Press
439 Kelley Drive
West Berlin, New Jersey 08091

Telephone: **800-772-6410**
Fax: **800-225-8894**
Email: **cs@townsendpress.com**
www.townsendpress.com

Table of Contents

A Note to Students............................. inside front cover

Introduction: Five Brief Stories 1

The Three Parts of This Book 8

Part 1: Bullying: The Hard Facts 9

Part 2: Real Stories about Bullies 15

    Bird Girl *Clark DeLeon*.. 16

    Rowing the Bus *Paul Langan* 25

    Two Lives Too Many *Peggy Kern*............................... 35

Part 3: What to Do about Bullying................................ 44

A Final Thought: Kindness Counts 71

Pledge to Stop Bullying 75

Bullying in Schools
What You Need to Know

There are many ways to hurt another human being. And there are some people—students you may know—who try their best to do just that. These kids are bullies, and each day they behave in ways that cause deep and lasting pain to others.

Here are five brief stories of bullying. They are all true, and there are countless other stories just like them.

Tarah

One afternoon, on the bus ride home from school, I watched Maribel, a high school junior, picking on Tarah, a ninth grader.

Maribel was shooting spitballs at Tarah's head. They were landing in wet clumps all over the place—on Tarah's seat, on her coat, in her hair. During this time, Tarah pretended to be asleep, but I knew she was awake. She was just too scared to do anything.

Maribel seemed to be annoyed that Tarah was not responding. She got up impulsively and started walking to the front of the bus. Other kids giggled as she crept up behind Tarah's seat. Then she pulled a pink glob of chewing gum from her mouth and shoved it deep into Tarah's long, curly hair. Kids at the back of the bus cheered as the gum clung to Tarah's scalp.

"Mar-i-BELL! Mar-i-BELL!"

During this whole time, Tarah didn't budge. She seemed frozen, as if she was somehow safer if she remained motionless. Yet everyone kept laughing and pointing to the neon pink mass tangled in her hair.

The next day, Tarah didn't come to school. When I saw her several days later, I noticed she avoided eye contact with me. And I could see that a section of her hair, roughly the size of the gum wad, had been cut out. Tarah tried to hide this by changing her hairstyle, but I knew what had happened. While I felt sorry for Tarah, I was grateful the older kids in the back of the bus had her to pick on instead of me.

Brian

Brian was a boy who followed me and my friends around when we were in sixth grade. Having been held back in school, he was a year older than the rest of us, and about six inches taller. His voice was loud and grating, and his insistence on being our friend irritated us. It didn't occur to me then how badly he must have needed a friend.

On the playground one winter day, we explained to Brian that we had thought of a new game. One of us would be the prisoner, while the rest of us would be divided into "prison guards" and "rescuers." Brian would have the honor of being the prisoner first. Excited to finally be part of our gang, he agreed. We collected all the jump ropes we could find and tied Brian to a tree at the very edge of the school property. Telling him that we would go organize ourselves into "guards" and "rescuers," we left him there. When the recess bell rang, we went to class. A teacher finally found Brian and untied him, and we were all called to the principal's office.

Instead of turning us in, Brian claimed that the whole game was his idea, and that he told us not to untie him because he wanted to escape on his own. He looked at the floor when he said this, and I could tell he was holding back tears. We were relieved not to get in trouble. But when Brian tried to play with us the next time, we chased him away.

Leslie Ann

Leslie stood out the second she got on the bus. Heavy-set with limp, greasy hair, she was so shy she couldn't even look at us. She would just sit there in her frumpy clothes barely saying a word. In class she was no better, keeping her eyes in her books and speaking only when teachers called on her.

One day in gym class, someone joked about how Leslie's thick body looked more like a man's than a girl's. That's when the rumors started that Leslie was gay. Soon people began joking about her name.

"Hey lesbian, I mean *Leslie Ann*, how come you're so quiet?"

The joke stuck. Soon it seemed everyone was calling her lesbian as if it was her name. Sometimes, when we were really bad, her face would get pink and blotchy like she was about to cry, but she never fought back except to say "stop" or "leave me alone." Most days, she pretended to ignore us, but you could tell she knew what we were saying. Then someone made up a story about how Leslie was spying on girls changing in the locker room. It spread all over school. One of my friends put a picture of Leslie on Facebook. It seemed like half the school wrote comments about her being gay. Even people who barely knew her were spreading rumors.

One afternoon, I saw her crying in the hallway. A teacher was asking her what was wrong but Leslie just kept sobbing and shaking her head. I knew the answer, and I felt bad, but I wasn't about to snitch on my classmates. After a few months, Leslie stopped coming to school. Someone said her mother decided to homeschool her, but someone else told me her parents split up and she moved in with her father.

I don't know what really happened. But I am certain of one thing: we had made Leslie's life miserable.

Rob

The bullies attacked me when I wasn't looking.

They'd been teasing me for days, calling me a "teacher's pet" ever since they learned I was on the Honor Roll. Normally I sat in the front of the bus and the bigger kids sat in the back. But on this day, the front seats were taken, and I had no choice but to sit closer to the bigger, louder kids.

I was 14, a skinny freshman in high school—the only freshman boy on the bus this particular day. Sitting in the back two rows were four seniors. They were big guys who liked to smoke; one even had a beard.

It happened quickly. I heard a voice shout "Hey, what's that?" and I turned. In a split second, two hands grabbed my shoulders and held them in place. Another kid sat in front of me so the bus driver couldn't see what was happening. A third grabbed my underwear from behind and yanked with all his might.

The pain was instant. The fabric of my shorts pulled tight and crushed my groin. Then it began to rip, forcing the cotton into uncomfortable places on my backside. Worse than the pain was the laughter. Everyone cackled as if the whole thing was a joke. But I wasn't laughing.

With a heave, he snapped the elastic strap, and a large section of my underwear came off in this kid's hand. He held it up like a trophy, and his friends cheered. Then he tied the torn strap around his forehead like a headband. Girls nearby clapped while the other boys relaxed their grip and shoved me into my seat.

I sat there trembling with anger and rage. If I had had a gun, I might have shot them all. "How dare they touch me!" I thought. "How dare everyone laugh!" But thankfully I had no gun, and the bus was stopping at my house.

"Look, he's going to cry," said the kid who tore my underwear. "Go ahead and cry, you little girl."

Sometimes today, years later, I still think about those boys and feel rage in my chest.

Shannon

In eighth grade, there was a new girl named Shannon in our class. She was very shy, very skinny, and her clothes were a bit out of style.

Within weeks of Shannon's arrival, a popular girl in our class started saying that Shannon had bad body odor. She claimed that Shannon smelled like "fish," and that she didn't clean herself. Before long, boys as well as girls joined in the teasing. They gave Shannon a nickname, "Seafood Shanty," after an actual restaurant in our neighborhood.

Soon people began making jokes about "crabs" whenever Shannon was around. Her face would get red, but she never said anything. Sometimes people pretended to be afraid of sitting next to her.

"Are you sure I gotta sit here? Something stinks!" they'd say if a teacher assigned them to a seat anywhere near Shannon. Boys claimed they saw shrimp and crabs crawling around under her desk. Some even called her "Sushi Shannon."

One day, one of my friends took a piece of chalk during lunchtime and drew a giant crab with the words "Now Available at Seafood Shanty" on the chalkboard. We all entered the class at the same time and read the sign. Everyone was laughing hysterically when Shannon walked in.

She looked at the chalkboard and the laughing faces around her—people enjoying her suffering—and she burst into tears. And then she did something that surprised me. She wailed out loud like a child in pain and ran out of the classroom.

Many people laughed even harder when she did that. I laughed, too. But deep inside, I knew we had gone too far. Still, I never had the guts to say anything. I wonder where Shannon is now.

Each of these stories is painful to read. But, sadly, such stories are very common. If your school is like most American schools, it's filled with people who have experienced or witnessed bullying. Perhaps that includes you.

According to the National Center for Education Statistics, nearly one-third of middle and high school students have experienced some kind of bullying. While this problem is more frequent among boys, about 1 in 4 girls from this same age group reports having at least one encounter with a bully. These interactions can be face to face, or they can happen electronically. In a recent study, 32% of teens said they've been bullied and harassed online or through text messages.

Look around. If your classroom contains 20 students, at least 6 of them—and most likely more—have dealt with bullies in one way or another. If you have not yet experienced this problem, you probably will.

What will you do? One thing is almost certain: at some point you'll have to make a choice about how to act in a bullying situation.

This booklet was written to help you prepare for your next encounter.

The Three Parts of this Book

Almost everyone agrees that bullying is wrong—even most bullies will admit this if you ask them privately. While knowledge alone does not seem to stop the problem, it's a start.

■ **PART ONE** of this book takes a close look at bullying to get a sense of what it is all about.

■ **PART TWO** provides true stories about bullies and their targets. These stories and the accompanying activities will help you walk in others' shoes and gain a deeper understanding of this widespread problem.

■ **PART THREE** presents ways to respond to bullying and cyberbullying situations.

ACTIVITY

Take ten or fifteen minutes to write about a bullying experience you've had. It could be a time when you witnessed a bully's attack or were more directly involved. Don't worry about grammar, punctuation, and spelling; just get your thoughts down on paper. Try to include details that help others see and hear what really happened. You may decide to end your paper by describing what the victim in the experience must have felt.

Writing will help get you thinking about your involvement with bullying. If you feel comfortable doing so, you might want to share what you've written with your peers. If not, keep your notes; you may be able to draw upon them for a writing assignment in Part 2.

Bullying is the deliberate and often repeated attempt to intimidate, embarrass, or harm another person. At its core, it involves the misuse of power. Those who bully typically have greater size, status, popularity, and control than their targets. They use each and sometimes all of these "strengths" as weapons against their more vulnerable peers. For years, bullying was dismissed as a normal part of growing up, something not to be taken seriously. Today, however, we know better.

Bullying is a serious and potentially deadly problem. On any given school day, approximately 160,000 kids skip school to avoid being picked on by their peers. A much larger number endure torment in silence. Children who are bullied are often too scared or anxious to focus on their school work, and their grades and test scores decline. Others experience stress-related illnesses including headaches, stomach troubles, panic attacks, and depression. In some cases, depression can be so severe that targets become suicidal, homicidal, or both. Research points to a significant link between bullying and the more than 4,000 teen suicides that occur yearly in the United States. Claims that bullying is harmless or just "kids being kids" could not be further from the truth.

Targets of Bullying

Anyone can be the target of bullying. Today it could be the new kid who just transferred to your school; tomorrow it could be you. Most bullies single out people who stand out in some way. But almost any quality—positive or negative—can become the focus of a bully's attention. If your grades are too high or too low, your style too different, your accent too foreign, your hair too long or too short, your body too big or too small, you may find yourself the target of a bully.

Witnesses of Bullying

Even if you have not been targeted by bullies, you have probably witnessed them in action. In most bullying situations, there are often more witnesses than there are bullies or targets. Ironically, these bystanders have the greatest power to determine what happens in school. Unfortunately, they usually don't use their power to stop bullying. Instead they often make it worse. Why?

A big reason is fear. Many who witness bullying choose to "stay out of it" because they are scared. They worry if they say something, the bully might turn on them. Others fear they might lose popularity if they intervene. Some are afraid they'll be labeled a "snitch" if they tell a teacher about the problem. For many students, this fear is so strong that they actually pretend to be friends with peers who bully. They may laugh at their jokes or join in their insults, becoming something of a bully themselves. Yet alone and away from the bully, these same people may be nice and friendly. Like targets, witnesses to bullying endure stress and fear as a result of what they see. Some may carry guilt for many years because they didn't help their peers. These kids are frightened bystanders, and schools everywhere—including yours—are filled with them.

Causes of Bullying

While there is no simple reason to explain why people become bullies, researchers have identified risk factors linked to this behavior. Young people with aggressive or impulsive personalities, for example, are more likely to bully. Physical size, especially among boys, can contribute to this problem, allowing bigger, aggressive children to dominate their smaller peers. However, size and personality alone do not make someone a bully.

Environmental factors can also influence bullying. Poor adult supervision in schools and communities increases the likelihood that bullying will take place. In addition, schools that lack violence-prevention programs or that do not deal effectively with bully-related incidents are more likely to experience bullying problems. Bullies thrive in environments where they are not held accountable for their behavior. This is one reason why the Internet, a place where identity is easily hidden, is so attractive to bullies.

Home environment also plays a significant role in bullying. Young people who spend long, unsupervised hours exposed to TV and video game violence are more likely to accept such behavior—and practice it. According to recent surveys, by the time the average American child is ten years old, he or she has witnessed thousands of acts of TV violence, including assault and murder. Video games intensify this exposure, encouraging kids to participate in aggressive and often brutal "play." Constant doses of this screen violence can make viewers less sensitive to the real thing. Because TV and video games hide the lasting pain that true violence causes, young people do not develop empathy and compassion for sufferers around them.

Exposure to *real* violence is another major factor in bullying. Research shows over and over that victims of bullies often become bullies. Whether they suffered at the hands of abusive family members or were tormented by other kids, bullies often copy the behaviors used against them. Their negative and hurtful experiences scar them and teach them a false and damaging lesson: to protect themselves, they must be mean to others.

Think about it: if a bully is the "toughest kid" in a classroom, who will pick on him? If she can come up with the cruelest insult or control "the crowd," who will dare stand up to her? In each case, bullying serves as a kind of armor. But instead of being a sign of strength, it is often a sign of deep hurt, insecurity, or fear. Look closely into the eyes of a bully, and you may be looking into the eyes of a former victim.

Yet these factors alone do not fully explain bullying. Not every bully has been victimized or suffers from poor self-esteem. Some appear to have a *strong* sense of self, perhaps too strong. They don't bully to feel better about themselves; they do it because they look down at their peers. For them, bullying is a way of showing superiority over those they consider physically and socially "beneath" them. Bullies with this view lack compassion for their peers and even go so far as to blame their targets for their attacks!

They are wrong. *All people—regardless of their background, race, religion, appearance, or sexual preference—deserve civility. Everyone has a right to be free from threats, intimidation, and cruelty.* This is particularly true for children, especially in school. For these and many other reasons, bullying cannot be tolerated. Reducing it is difficult, but it can be done. Many schools have succeeded in doing so. Yours can too.

To begin reducing this problem, however, you must first understand it.

Types of Bullying

Research tells us that bullying is most common in grades 6 to 10, but it can happen at nearly any age and among both sexes. While it takes many forms, bullying usually involves several kinds of behavior.

Among boys, *physical bullying* seems to be the typical method of attack. Pushing, tripping, and hitting are widespread and well-known examples of this type of behavior. Among girls, however, social bullying dominates.

Social or *relational bullying* is the use of peer pressure and manipulation to isolate a target and hurt his or her feelings. A social bully may, for example, convince an entire group of people to ignore, shun, or avoid a particular student. Those who endure this type of attack often feel trapped in an invisible cage—one in which they have no friends, no one to talk to, and no way to escape.

Just as painful—and perhaps most common—is *verbal bullying*. This occurs when bullies tease, mock, threaten, insult, and taunt their peers. Verbal attacks also include spreading rumors, gossip, and lies. Often these false stories are passed rapidly by word of mouth. Designed to be as hurtful as possible, verbal attacks usually focus on things outside their target's control, such as physical appearance, race, family, or parents' income. Insults of this type may also focus on a target's sexuality or spread lies about his or her sexual history. Verbal bullying disproves the old saying that "sticks and stones break bones, but names can never hurt." Cruel words *do* hurt. They cause immense pain, embarrassment, and shame to those who are targeted.

When verbal and social bullying take place over the Internet or an electronic device, they become something else: *cyberbullying*. Cell phones, instant messages, social networking sites, website chat rooms, and even online video games are the spaces where this growing form of bullying strikes. Using this technology, bullies have been able to intensify and spread their attacks on a scale that wasn't possible years ago. Targets of cyberbullying are caught in a real-life nightmare, surrounded by people online *and* in person who torment them. As with other forms of bullying, many know who is responsible for the attacks but refuse to get involved for fear that they will lose popularity or suffer the same abuse. As a result, the targets end up alone and isolated at a time when friends and support are most needed.

Some forms of bullying—including cyberbullying—actually involve criminal behavior. Bullies who vandalize property, take lunch money, make threats, steal someone's online identity, spread inappropriate photos, or post someone else's private information on the Internet are committing acts that are not just hurtful; they are crimes. In fact, about 25% of school-age bullies end up with criminal records before they reach the age of 30. Bullies are also often the instigators—and victims—of school violence. School shootings in a number of states (most notably the 1999 massacre at Columbine High School in Littleton, Colorado) can be traced directly to bullying.

The message is loud and clear: bullying is no laughing matter. It deserves your attention right now. As a student in school today, you are on the front lines of this problem.

ACTIVITY

Take a minute or two to get a quick sense of bullying at your school.

■ How many actual bullies do you know of at your school right now?

___ none

___ 1-5

___ more than 5

■ How many targets of bullies do you know of right now?

___ none

___ 1-5

___ more than 5

■ How many frightened bystanders do you know of right now?

___ none

___ 1-5

___ more than 5

PART 2:
REAL STORIES ABOUT BULLIES

Three real-life accounts of bullies follow: **"Bird Girl"** by Clark DeLeon, **"Rowing the Bus"** by Paul Langan, and **"Two Lives Too Many"** by Peggy Kern.

As you read each essay, think of your own experiences with bullying. What would you do if you witnessed similar events in your own school? How would you want others to respond if you were being targeted? If you are comfortable doing so, share your thoughts with your classmates and your teacher when you discuss each reading.

Bird Girl
Clark DeLeon

Preview

"Sticks and stones can break my bones, but names can never hurt me." Is this old saying true? Or can teasing hurt, and hurt deeply? In the following selection, made up of three columns first published in the Philadelphia Inquirer, *Clark DeLeon writes about the lasting scars—and tragedies—that can result from childhood teasing, and his readers respond.*

Targets: A Lesson in Life

There was a weird girl in my high school whom we all called the Bird. We called her that because of her nervous, birdlike movements and the way she would hunch her shoulders toward her ears as if she was hoping her head would disappear into her body. She had sallow skin that looked as if it had never felt the sun, and there was usually a blotchy red rash in the middle of her forehead. She had fine black hair on her arms long enough to comb, and she wore clothes that had [long] been out of fashion. . . . She was also the object of such contempt and scorn, such cruel ridicule, that it shames me to this day to think I was part of it.

Oh, I was never one to say anything to her face. I wasn't that brave. I'd wait until she hurried by with her books held tightly to her chest and join in the chorus of birdcalls with the other guys. She was always good for a laugh. And it's important when you're a teenager to join the laughter, or the laughter might turn on you.

I remember one day when the Bird was surrounded by three or four popular guys who had stopped her in the corridor between classes. They were flapping their arms and screeching in her ear. She was terrified. Her eyes darted in panic. A couple of her books fell to the floor. When she stopped to pick them up, they bent over her in a circle, closing in, screeching, screeching.

Then this girl came out of nowhere. I'd never seen such anger in a girl before. She went up to the leader of the tormentors and ripped into him with a hot fury. "Stop it!" she shouted. "Can't you see what you're doing?" The guys backed off, stunned. Then the girl went over to the Bird and put her arm around her shoulder and walked her to class.

I thought about the Bird when I read about Nathan Faris, the little boy who shot a classmate and killed himself after being the target of teasing by the kids in his school. I thought of how I had been a part of her misery, how more than 20 years later it still bothers me. But I also think of what I learned that day about decency and bravery, about being a human being, from a girl whose name I don't even know. And I wonder if that one act of bold kindness may have saved another girl's life.

Targets: Why Are Kids So Cruel?

"I just had to write to you in regard to your item 'Targets' that appeared in today's (March 8) *Inquirer,*" wrote Ray Windsor of Lansdowne.

I received several letters about that piece, which concerned a girl I knew in high school who was the victim of cruel and unrelenting ridicule because she was unattractive, uncool and unable to defend herself. That piece touched a chord in people, and I think Ray's story will, too. Here it is:

"Back in high school I had to contend with many of the malicious deeds and taunts from my 'fellow students,' similar but different. With me, however, I was a victim of gross physical immaturity. . . . I actually didn't start shaving regularly until I was 25 or so.

"This problem was very hard for me to deal with, even though it was out of my control. The class 'bullies' and insensitive and uncaring types never hesitated for one moment to knock me around, having read my problems like a book. Gym class, especially, was my psychological encounter with hell— twice weekly. Because of my outward appearance, I always skipped showering with the rest of the class. Eventually, they caught on to this and many of the guys would either throw me in the showers, or if they didn't do this, they would spit in my underwear or socks or shoes and then (usually) chuck them out of the window to the ground two stories below.

"Is it no wonder I was sick as often as I could be on Gym Day? Oh, all the wonderful FUN they had at my emotional expense. I once mustered the courage to talk to my 'guidance counselor' about the problems I was contending with, and all he was able to tell me was that this was the type of thing that students like myself go through to become a man. How I was to become a man through all this escaped me, primarily because I was being treated as less than human by these jerks.

"Once this pattern was set up, I easily became a target for much the same outside of gym. Often I was pushed and shoved in the hallway. On occasion, I was tripped or punched, and on special occasions, I would even be tossed into the movable trash cans and rolled into classrooms that weren't even mine. I may have been bigger than some of these bullies, but I could never seem to get the courage to bring a fist up to their ugly faces. It was always THEM against ME. How often I broke down and cried out of sheer frustration is uncountable. What really gets me is that I let this happen. Is it any wonder that I turned to alcohol and had two major ulcer operations before I was 25?

"As I suspect you know by now, I have picked up the shattered pieces of my adolescence and have gotten my life back together again. The HATE and RAGE I once felt for these ne'er-do-wells has since turned to pity. In fact, they are no doubt half-decent guys now. But if they only knew how much harm they'd caused me, they'd become a little upset with themselves. At least I hope so, anyway. I only wish that someone had yelled 'Stop it! Can't you see what you're doing?' back at school. It may have saved me from much of the misery I was forced to endure until I graduated from that hell hole."

That's Ray's story. I've got my own, and you probably have yours.

How did we survive those years? How did we endure the anger, the shame, the emotional brutality? And we're talking middle-class suburban kids, here. We're talking the seeds of the promised land. If parents only knew what their kids were going through, what their kids are going through.

I don't know if there's an answer. How can we make teenagers treat each other like human beings? How can we penetrate that closed society of adolescence? How can we let the victims know that life gets better? How can we shame the bullies with what they will feel about their actions, if they ever grow up?

Kids: Lessons Learned Early

I want to share something with you, something nice.

It's what some kids have had to say in letters to me about the column about the Bird, the girl I knew in high school who was teased and tormented by everyone, until one day another girl stood up to a group of guys who were picking on the Bird. You wonder when you write something like this about growing up, how kids will receive your message. Here are some of their reactions:

"I read your article about the weird girl called the Bird," wrote Stephanie K. "I am in the sixth grade, and one of my classmates is weird like in your article, and we too make fun of him. We don't make fun of him as much anymore. We used to make fun of him all day long. . . . I really thought about what you've said and I want to thank you for taking time to write something that will prevent other people from feeling bad."

"I have read your story about the girl that was called the Bird because she had pale skin and acted weird. In the story, you said that you were one of the ones who teased the Bird," wrote

Cuong N. "You also spoke highly of the girl who came up to you and your friends and told you guys to stop teasing the Bird. If you spoke highly of that girl, why didn't you do the same thing, or were you scared of being teased too? If I was in your place, I would have done the same thing you did and prevented myself from being teased. Please write back to me if you can."

"I would probably have done the same thing as you did," wrote Katie M. "Now that I read the story and understand the problem going on, I wonder why more people aren't like the kid who came and helped the Bird."

"I think the girl who stood up for the Bird was very brave," wrote Nicole G. "She could have been beaten up or teased, but she did it anyway. I really look up to and respect people like that."

"I think that you shouldn't have held back what you thought about the other kids teasing the Bird, because that makes you in a way worse than the others," wrote Michael C. "If you felt that the girl reacted bravely for sticking up for the Bird and that she was a good person for doing what she did, why didn't you at least find out who she was?"

I wish I had found out her name, Michael. And I respect people like that too, Nicole. And I too wonder why more people aren't like the girl who helped the Bird, Katie. And the reason I spoke highly of the girl is that I was afraid to do what she did, and her bravery inspired me, Cuong. And I'm especially glad that you've stopped teasing your sixth-grade classmate, Stephanie. Thank you all for thinking about the story the way you did.

A QUICK READING CHECK

Below are five questions that provide a quick review of the selection's content. Circle the answer that best completes each question.

1. Which sentence best expresses the central point of DeLeon's "Bird Girl"?
   a. Gym class is the worst place for teenagers who are victims of teasing.
   b. Childhood and adolescence are difficult times for many people.
   c. A classmate's courageous action may have saved a girl's life.
   d. Young people should learn to stop being cruel to people who are different.

2. When DeLeon was a student, how did he treat the Bird?
   a. He teased her openly to her face.
   b. He tried to defend her when others treated her cruelly.
   c. He avoided teasing her because he believed it was wrong.
   d. He joined in the crowds that teased and laughed at her.

3. The most humiliating experiences for Ray Windsor took place in
   a. math class.
   b. the cafeteria.
   c. gym class.
   d. English class.

4. After reading DeLeon's article, a student named Stephanie K. wrote that
   a. she thought DeLeon was in a way worse than the other students who had teased the Bird.
   b. she looked up to people like the girl who had defended the Bird.
   c. DeLeon should have found out the name of the girl who had defended the Bird.
   d. she and her friends are now teasing a "weird" classmate less often.

5. The author suggests that Nathan Faris
   a. might have been helped like the Bird if someone had stood up for him.
   b. was probably very different from the Bird.
   c. was justified in shooting one of his classmates.
   d. was too weak to defend himself.

QUESTIONS TO THINK ABOUT

The four questions that follow provide you and your classmates with an opportunity to further your understanding of the selection. Your teacher may ask you to respond to these questions individually or in small groups as well as in a large classroom setting.

1. Many centuries ago the Greek philosopher Philo of Alexandria made the following observation: "Be kind, for everyone you meet is fighting a great battle." What do you think he meant by this statement? How might it apply to "Bird Girl"?

2. In the second paragraph, DeLeon says that "it's important when you're a teenager to join the laughter, or the laughter might turn on you." What does he mean? Is he correct?

3. Why do you think so many readers wrote to DeLeon about the story of the Bird?

4. DeLeon asks, "How can we make teenagers treat each other like human beings?" How would you answer this question?

TOPICS TO WRITE ABOUT

Below are three writing assignments based on the situations and ideas in DeLeon's essay. Each invites you to put your thoughts about bullying into writing.

1. **Writing a Script:** Some students find themselves making the bold decision to confront a bully. Write the script for a conversation in which a student confronts his or her bully. The following is the format for writing a script:

   Alex: Well, look who it is! Little ugly Carla. You're so ugly. . .

   Carla: Stop! I've had enough of your bullying! I want you to stop right now.

   Try to make the conversation as realistic as possible. What kinds of things would the characters say to each other? How would they go about resolving this problem, if at all? Try to express, through their words, the kinds of emotions they are feeling.

   Begin your script with a narrator who explains who the characters are, what they are doing, and where they are when the conversation takes place.

   Your script might then be performed in class, with one student as the narrator, another as the bully's victim, and a third student as the bully.

2. **Writing a Paragraph:** Write a paragraph about a person who was teased or bullied in your school or neighborhood. Describe the person and then explain how others treated him or her. Make your description detailed enough so that your readers can picture the person clearly and understand what happened. Use a topic sentence such as "Gordon was bullied a lot by my eighth-grade classmates because of his unusual behavior."

3. **Writing an Essay:** When Ray Windsor went to his school guidance counselor to talk about being teased, he didn't receive much help. What would you do if you were a counselor who was asked to come up with ideas to help students treat one another better? Write an essay in which you make detailed suggestions for what teachers and students could do to make your school a friendlier, gentler place. You might want to include such ideas as an anti-teasing education campaign, a student and teacher discussion group, or a buddy system, in which older students act as personal counselors to younger students.

Rowing the Bus

Paul Langan

Preview

If you could go back in time and undo one thing you are sorry for, what would it be? Such a long-regretted moment is the focus of Paul Langan's essay. While we can never turn back the clock, this story illustrates how we can do the next best thing: we can turn our regrets into valuable lessons in living.

When I was in elementary school, some older kids made me row the bus. Rowing meant that on the way to school I had to sit in the dirty bus aisle littered with paper, gum wads, and spitballs. Then I had to simulate the motion of rowing while the kids around me laughed and chanted, "Row, row, row the bus." I was forced to do this by a group of bullies who spent most of their time picking on me.

I was the perfect target for them. I was small. I had no father. And my mother, though she worked hard to support me, was unable to afford clothes and sneakers that were "cool." Instead she dressed me in outfits that we got from "the bags"—hand-me-downs given as donations to a local church.

Each Wednesday, she'd bring several bags of clothes to the house and pull out musty, wrinkled shirts and worn bell-bottom pants that other families no longer wanted. I knew that people were kind to give things to us, but I hated wearing clothes that might have been donated by my classmates. Each time I wore something from the bags, I feared that the other kids might recognize something that was once theirs.

Besides my outdated clothes, I wore thick glasses, had crossed eyes, and spoke with a persistent lisp. For whatever reason, I had never learned to say the "s" sound properly, and I pronounced words that began with "th" as if they began with a "d." In addition, because of my severely crossed eyes, I lacked the hand and eye coordination necessary to hit or catch flying objects.

As a result, footballs, baseballs, soccer balls and basketballs became my enemies. I knew, before I stepped onto the field or court, that I would do something clumsy or foolish and that everyone would laugh at me. I feared humiliation so much that I became skillful at feigning illnesses to get out of gym class. Eventually I learned how to give myself low-grade fevers so the nurse would write me an excuse. It worked for a while, until the gym teachers caught on. When I did have to play, I was always the last one chosen to be on any team. In fact, team captains did everything in their power to make their opponents get stuck with me. When the unlucky team captain was forced to call my name, I would trudge over to the team, knowing that no one there liked or wanted me. For four years, from second through fifth grade, I prayed nightly for God to give me school days in which I would not be insulted, embarrassed, or made to feel ashamed.

I thought my prayers were answered when my mother decided to move during the summer before sixth grade. The move meant that I got to start sixth grade in a different school, a place where I had no reputation. Although the older kids laughed and snorted at me as soon as I got on my new bus— they couldn't miss my thick glasses and strange clothes—I soon discovered that there was another kid who received the brunt of their insults. His name was George, and everyone made fun of him. The kids taunted him because he was skinny; they belittled him because he had acne that pocked and blotched his face, and they teased him because his voice was squeaky. During my first gym class at my new school, I wasn't the last one chosen for kickball; George was.

George tried hard to be friends with me, coming up to me in the cafeteria on the first day of school. "Hi. My name's George. Can I sit with you?" he asked with a peculiar squeakiness that made each word high-pitched and raspy. As I nodded for him to sit down, I noticed an uncomfortable silence in the cafeteria. Many of the students who had mocked George's clumsiness during gym class were watching the two of us and whispering among themselves. By letting him sit with me, I had violated an unspoken law of school, a sinister code of childhood that demands there must always be someone to pick on. I began to realize two things. If I befriended George, I would soon receive the same treatment that I had gotten at my old school. If I stayed away from him, I might actually have a chance to escape being at the bottom.

Within days, the kids started taunting us whenever we were together. "Who's your new little buddy, Georgie?" In the hallways, groups of students began mumbling just loud enough for me to hear, "Look, it's George's ugly boyfriend." On the bus rides to and from school, wads of paper and wet chewing gum were tossed at me by the bigger, older kids in the back of the bus.

It became clear that my friendship with George was going to cause me several more years of misery at my new school. I decided to stop being friends with George. In class and at lunch, I spent less and less time with him. Sometimes I told him I was too busy to talk; other times I acted distracted and gave one-word responses to whatever he said. Our classmates, sensing that they had created a rift between George and me, intensified their attacks on him. Each day, George grew more desperate as he realized that the one person who could prevent him from being completely isolated was closing him off. I knew that I shouldn't avoid him, that he was feeling the same way I felt for so long, but I was so afraid that my life would become the hell it had been in my old school that I continued to ignore him.

Then, at recess one day, the meanest kid in the school, Chris, decided he had had enough of George. He vowed that he was going to beat up George and anyone else who claimed to be his friend. A mob of kids formed and came after me. Chris led the way and cornered me near our school's swing sets. He grabbed me by my shirt and raised his fist over my head. A huge gathering of kids surrounded us, urging him to beat me up, chanting "Go, Chris, go!"

"You're Georgie's new little boyfriend, aren't you?" he yelled. The hot blast of his breath carried droplets of his spit into my face. In a complete betrayal of the only kid who was nice to me, I denied George's friendship.

"No, I'm not George's friend. I don't like him. He's stupid," I blurted out. Several kids snickered and mumbled under their breath. Chris stared at me for a few seconds and then threw me to the ground.

"Wimp. Where's George?" he demanded, standing over me. Someone pointed to George sitting alone on top of the monkey bars about thirty yards from where we were. He was watching me. Chris and his followers sprinted over to George and yanked him off the bars to the ground. Although the mob quickly encircled them, I could still see both boys at the center of the crowd, looking at each other. George seemed strangely frozen, staring straight through Chris. I heard the familiar chant of "Go, Chris, go!" and watched as his fists began slamming into George's head and body. His face bloodied and his nose broken, George crumpled to the ground and sobbed without having even thrown a punch. The mob cheered with pleasure and darted off into the playground to avoid an approaching teacher.

Chris was suspended, and after a few days, George came back to school. I wanted to talk to him, to ask him how he was, to apologize for leaving him alone and for not trying to stop him from getting hurt. But I couldn't go near him. Filled with shame for denying George and angered by my own cowardice, I never spoke to him again.

Several months later, without telling any students, George transferred to another school. Once in a while, in those last weeks before he left, I caught him watching me as I sat with the rest of the kids in the cafeteria. He never yelled at me or expressed anger, disappointment, or even sadness. Instead he just looked at me.

In the years that followed, George's silent stare remained

with me. It was there in eighth grade when I saw a gang of popular kids beat up a sixth-grader because, they said, he was "ugly and stupid." It was there my first year in high school, when I saw a group of older kids steal another freshman's clothes and throw them into the showers. It was there a year later, when I watched several seniors press a wad of chewing gum into the hair of a new girl on the bus. Each time that I witnessed another awkward, uncomfortable, scared kid being tormented, I thought of George, and gradually his haunting stare began to speak to me. No longer silent, it told me that every child who is picked on and taunted deserves better, that no one—no matter how big, strong, attractive, or popular—has the right to abuse another person.

Finally, in my junior year when a loudmouthed, pink-skinned bully named Donald began picking on two freshmen on the bus, I could no longer deny George. Donald was crumpling a large wad of paper and preparing to bounce it off the back of the head of one of the young students when I interrupted him.

"Leave them alone, Don," I said. By then I was six inches taller and, after two years of high-school wrestling, thirty pounds heavier than I had been in my freshman year. Though Donald was a year older than me, he wasn't much bigger. He stopped what he was doing, squinted and stared at me.

"What's your problem, Paul?"

I felt the way I had many years earlier when I watched the mob of kids begin to surround George on the playground.

"Just leave them alone. They aren't bothering you," I responded quietly.

"What's it to you?" he challenged. A glimpse of my own past, of rowing the bus, of being mocked for my clothes, my lisp, my glasses, and my absent father flashed in my mind.

"Just don't mess with them. That's all I am saying, Don." My fingertips were tingling. The bus was silent. He got up from his seat and leaned over me, and I rose from my seat to face him.

For a minute, both of us just stood there, without a word, staring.

"I'm just playing with them, Paul," he said, chuckling. "You don't have to go psycho on me or anything." Then he shook his head, slapped me firmly on the chest with the back of his hand, and sat down. But he never threw that wad of paper. For the rest of the year, whenever I was on the bus, Don and the other troublemakers were noticeably quiet.

Although it has been years since my days on the playground and the school bus, George's look still haunts me. Today, I see it on the faces of a few scared kids at my sister's school—she is in fifth grade. Or once in a while I'll catch a glimpse of someone like George on the evening news, in a story about a child who brought a gun to school to stop the kids from picking on him, or in a feature about a teenager who killed herself because everyone teased her. In each school, in almost every classroom, there is a George, hoping that someone nearby will be strong enough to be kind and brave enough to stand up against people who attack, tease, or hurt those who are vulnerable.

If asked about their behavior, the bullies would probably say, "What's it to you? It's just a joke. It's nothing." But to George and me, and everyone else who has been humiliated or laughed at or spat on, it is everything. No one should have to row the bus.

A QUICK READING CHECK

Below are five questions that provide a quick review of the selection's content. Circle the answer that best completes each question.

1. Which sentence best expresses the central point of Langan's essay?
   a. Although Paul Langan was a target of other students' abuse when he was a young boy, their attacks stopped as he grew taller and stronger.
   b. When Langan moved to a different school, he discovered that another student, George, was the target of more bullying than he was.
   c. Langan's experience of being bullied and his shame at how he treated George eventually made him speak up for someone else who was teased.
   d. Langan is ashamed that he did not stand up for George when George was being attacked by a bully on the playground.

2. When Chris attacked George, George reacted by
   a. fighting back hard.
   b. shouting for Langan to help him.
   c. running away.
   d. accepting the beating.

3. Langan finally found the courage to stand up for abused students when he saw
   a. Donald about to throw paper at a younger student.
   b. older kids throwing a freshman's clothes into the shower.
   c. seniors putting bubble gum in a new student's hair.
   d. a gang beating up a sixth-grader whom they disliked.

4. We can conclude that when Langan began sixth grade at the new school, he
   a. became quite popular.
   b. began to dress more fashionably.
   c. was relieved to find someone who was more unpopular than he was.
   d. became a bully himself.

5. The author implies that
   a. the kids who picked on George did not really intend to be cruel.
   b. bullying can lead to terrible tragedies at schools.
   c. his sister is the victim of teasing, much as he was.
   d. George grew up to be a confident, well-adjusted person.

QUESTIONS TO THINK ABOUT

The four questions that follow provide you and your classmates with an opportunity to further your understanding of the selection. Your teacher may ask you to respond to these questions individually or in small groups as well as in a large classroom setting.

1. Paul Langan titled his selection "Rowing the Bus." Yet very little of the essay actually deals with the incident the title describes—only the first and last paragraphs. Why do you think Langan chose that title?

2. Langan wanted to be kind to George, but he wanted even more to be accepted by the other students. Have you ever found yourself in a similar situation—where you wanted to do the right thing but felt that it had too high a price? Explain what happened.

3. Langan refers to "a sinister code of childhood that demands there must always be someone to pick on." What does the phrase "a sinister code of childhood" mean to you? Why do children need someone to pick on?

4. The novelist Henry James once said, "Three things in human life are important. The first is to be kind. The second is to be kind. And the third is to be kind." Are there things that teachers, school administrators, parents, and other concerned adults can do to encourage young people to treat one another with kindness rather than cruelty?

TOPICS TO WRITE ABOUT

Below are three writing assignments based on the situations and ideas in Langan's essay. Each invites you to put your thoughts about bullying into writing.

1. **Writing a Script:** Bullying happens each day because bystanders refuse to get involved when they see it taking place. Write the script for an encounter in which a person witnesses a bully in action and decides to take a stand. The following is the format for writing a script:

   Ralph: Here comes pizza face again. Last time I saw something that greasy, it had cheese on it.

   Keisha: Leave him alone. He ain't bothering you.

   Try to make the conversation as realistic as possible. What exactly would the characters say to each other? What, if anything, could they say to resolve their situation? Try to express, through the characters' words, the kinds of emotions they are feeling.

   Begin your script with a narrator who explains who the characters are, what they are doing, and where they are when the conversation takes place.

   Your script might then be performed in class, with one student as the narrator, another as the bully, and a third as the person who steps in to stop the bully. You might also want to include a fourth student to be the bully's victim.

2. **Writing a Paragraph:** Because he feared how other students would treat him, Langan decided to stop being friends with George. How do you feel about his decision? Do you think it was cruel? Understandable? Were there other options Langan might have tried? Write a paragraph in which you explain what you think of Langan's decision and why. Suggest at least one other way he could have acted, and tell what you think the consequences might have been.

3. **Writing an Essay:** Based on reading this essay, and on your own observations, can you pick out several characteristics that many bullies share? Write an essay that supports this thesis statement: "Most bullies share certain characteristics." In your essay, discuss two or three qualities of bullies, devoting a paragraph to each quality. Support your claim with evidence from the essay or from your own experience. In your concluding paragraph, you might discuss what these characteristics tell us about bullies.

Two Lives Too Many
Peggy Kern

Preview

"It was only a joke." Those who bully often say this when confronted about their behavior. This is especially true with cyberbullying. A text or instant message may seem less serious than a punch. But as Peggy Kern's essay shows, cyberbullying can be as devastating as the cruelest face-to-face attack—and the consequences just as tragic.

Thirteen-year-old Megan Meier couldn't believe her good luck.

"Mom! Mom! Mom! Look at him!" Megan exclaimed. Her eyes sparkled with excitement. "He's *hot*!"

"Do you know who he is?" Megan's mother asked.

His name was Josh Evans. He was 16 years old. And he had sent Megan a friend request on MySpace.

"Please, can I add him?" Megan begged. "Please!"

Megan's mother agreed. She'd kept a close eye on Megan's MySpace activity, and she and Megan's father knew their daughter's password. Megan could not log on without their permission.

Megan's mother was glad to see her daughter so excited. Megan hadn't always had an easy life. She was a heavy girl and had struggled to lose weight for years. She also battled depression. But things were getting better. Megan had just started eighth grade at a new middle school. She'd lost 20 pounds and joined the volleyball team. She'd also ended a stormy friendship with a girl who lived up the block.

For the next six weeks, under her mother's watchful eye, Megan and Josh got to know each other. Josh said he was homeschooled. His parents were divorced and he'd just moved to town with his mom and two brothers. The family struggled for money.

"When i was 7 my dad left me and my mom and my older brother and my newborn brother 3 boys god i know poor mom yeah she had such a hard time when we were younger finding work to pay for us after he left," Josh wrote in an email.

Megan seemed happy—and much of her happiness came from talking with her new friend, a cute boy who seemed to understand her. Each day after school she'd rush home to check her computer to see if Josh had written her.

Megan's mother kept tabs on their conversations. She noticed Josh was always polite, but he never wanted to speak to Megan on the phone. He also made excuses when Megan asked for his phone number. Still, he was never rude, and Megan seemed thrilled about their blossoming friendship.

Then suddenly, on a Sunday in October, Josh sent Megan a disturbing message.

"I don't know if I want to be friends with you anymore because I've heard that you are not very nice to your friends," he wrote.

Confused, Megan fired off a quick reply. "What are you talking about?" she wrote. But Josh did not respond.

Then on Monday, Megan came home from school to find that Josh had sent her more troubling messages. But that wasn't the worst of it. To her horror, he had also shared some of Megan's private messages with other people online.

Who was this boy? Why was he doing this to her?

Megan's mother was in a rush to take her other daughter to the doctor. She ordered Megan to log off of MySpace until she returned. But a few minutes later, she received a frantic call from Megan. She was being verbally attacked, not just by Josh but by a large group of people. Suddenly Megan had become the target of an angry gang of invisible faces that seemed intent on burning her to the ground. She was called a "slut" and "fat." Surveys were posted asking cruel, embarrassing questions about her. And Josh continued to send her nasty messages.

Megan's mother pleaded with Megan to turn off the computer.

"No, mom. They are all being so mean to me!" Megan wept. When her mother and sister returned from the doctor appointment, Megan fled to her room in tears.

What had Megan felt that night, alone in her dark room? How did she make sense of what had happened? Josh turning on her. Her private messages made public. An unending stream of online insults. The betrayal of a boy she liked and trusted.

Megan must have been in agony. She'd been attacked not just by strangers, but by someone she trusted and cared about. She'd been so nice to Josh. Up until that Sunday, things had seemed perfect. He thought she was cool, and she dared to believe him. And perhaps, tragically, she also believed his final message to her, a message her parents would not find until it was too late. It read, in part:

"You are a bad person and everybody hates you. . . . The world would be a better place without you."

Megan took her life that night, hanging herself in her closed bedroom. She died believing Josh Evans was a real boy.

In truth, he never existed.

A group of girls from Megan's neighborhood had created a fake profile to trick Megan. The goal was to gain Megan's trust—to make her believe that "Josh" liked her—and then use that information to humiliate her online.

The girls eventually shared the password to the "Josh Evans" profile with other kids, encouraging them to participate in the joke. Slowly, over the course of six weeks, they gained Megan's trust. On the night she killed herself, they all took turns attacking Megan. They thought it was hilarious.

While their intention was not to drive Megan to suicide, that is how their cruel joke ended. Maybe Megan was more vulnerable than other kids. She did struggle with low self-esteem. She was heavy and sometimes, very, very sad. Perhaps that made her an easy target, and it could have made her more fragile than others facing the same kind of cruelty.

But if the attacks and lies had never happened, Megan would not have endured the despair that overwhelmed her during her final hours. If the attacks had never happened, she might still be with us today.

Tragically, Megan's story is not unique. John Halligan knows this. His son Ryan committed suicide after enduring months of cyberbullying attacks from his classmates.

John ransacked his son's room the day after Ryan's death searching for answers. He emptied drawers, rifled through notebooks, and tore apart the closet. He searched every pocket and opened every box. He was desperate to find something—a note, a diary, *anything*—that would explain why his 13-year-old son was dead.

Then he spotted Ryan's computer.

"I logged onto Ryan's AOL account and instantly received dozens of responses. First, they wanted to know why I was using Ryan's account," John remembers. "Well, I wanted to know if anyone was willing to share information with me—then the mystery began to unravel."

Ryan was a sweet and gentle kid, a lanky boy with brown hair who liked to swim, bike, camp, and play computer games. In some ways, Ryan was a typical 13-year-old. But in other ways, Ryan was different. As a young child, he was diagnosed with a learning disability. He struggled in school and attended Special Education classes until the fifth grade. He also had trouble with his motor skills. As a result, Ryan was uncoordinated and physically weaker than the other boys at school.

Ryan was bullied for the first time in fifth grade. One kid in particular began to tease him for being clumsy and "slow." John encouraged his son to ignore the bully, but the taunts continued. Others had joined in, too. Finally, in seventh grade Ryan asked his father to teach him self-defense. John agreed and soon after, Ryan and the bully had a fight at a local park. Ryan was proud of himself for landing a few punches. The strategy seemed to work: The bully backed off and the boys even became friendly.

But then, as John learned through Ryan's online friends, towards the end of the school year, someone started a rumor that Ryan was gay. The story sparked a feeding frenzy. Ryan was teased and ridiculed every day at school. At home, the attacks continued late into the evening as Ryan sat alone in his room at the computer. He was now the target of an online bullying campaign that continued well into the summer. Hour after hour, Ryan was called a "fag," "loser," and worse. Ryan's former nemesis—the boy he'd fought at the park—was one of the ringleaders.

This time, Ryan could not use his fists to defend himself. He could not fight off so many people at once. Already broken and humiliated, the final blow came when a popular girl began to flirt with Ryan online. She convinced Ryan she had a crush on him. But when school began and Ryan approached her in person, she told him it was all a joke. In front of her friends, she laughed and called him a loser.

Ryan was crushed.

"It's girls like you who make me want to kill myself," he told her. On October 7th, he did just that.

In the weeks following his son's death, John would find folder after folder of conversations that Ryan had saved on his computer. They show Ryan's desperate attempts to defend himself against the cyberbullying. Over time, more of Ryan's classmates came forward to tell what they knew. It appears that nearly all of the students at Ryan's school were aware of the bullying campaign. Almost no one defended him while it was happening.

"Clearly I made a mistake putting that computer in Ryan's room," Ryan's father admits. "Ryan had these online relationships that were invisible to me." In hindsight, he wishes he'd kept a closer eye on Ryan. He wishes Ryan had confided in him. But what about those who *did* know? Those who stood by and said nothing? Would Ryan have survived if more people had spoken up on his behalf?

Ryan was a sweet and gentle kid, a 13-year-old boy who, just like Megan Meier, was far too young to die.

Sadly, while you're reading this essay, cyberbullying continues. It's even more common now than when Ryan and

Megan were at school. Young people will experience it today. Perhaps they are in your community, your school, or even your class. If you see them, remember Megan and Ryan. And stand up for your peers.

A QUICK READING CHECK

Below are five questions that provide a quick review of the selection's content. Circle the answer that best completes each question.

1. Which sentence best expresses the central point of Kern's essay?
   a. Megan and Ryan's parents were unaware of the difficulty their children were enduring in school.
   b. Megan was happy when she started eighth grade at a new middle school and met Josh online.
   c. Cyberbullying contributed to the suicides of Megan and Ryan and remains a serious problem for school students.
   d. After fighting with a rival classmate, Ryan seemed to resolve his problems with a kid who once bullied him.

2. When Megan's mother first learned of Josh, she
   a. refused to let Megan talk to him.
   b. gave her permission to talk to him.
   c. left to take Megan's sister to the doctor.
   d. told Megan to turn off her computer.

3. Ryan's response to the bullies he encountered in seventh grade was to
   a. ask his father to teach him self-defense to protect himself.
   b. hide from his father the truth about what he was facing.
   c. tell a fellow classmate of the problems he was having in school.
   d. refuse to use his computer so bullies couldn't target him.

4. In both Megan and Ryan's case, cyberbullies
   a. were complete strangers to their targets.
   b. acted alone to humiliate their targets.
   c. knew their targets and were joined by others.
   d. encountered others who disapproved of their actions.

5. Based on the two stories in Kern's essay, we can conclude that
   a. cyberbullying attacks are at least as painful as other forms of bullying.
   b. cyberbullying attacks are often something many young people know about and participate in.
   c. cyberbullyng attacks can be continuous and wear down their targets over time.
   d. all of the above.

QUESTIONS TO THINK ABOUT

The four questions that follow provide you and your classmates with an opportunity to further your understanding of the selection. Your teacher may ask you to respond to these questions individually or in small groups as well as in a large classroom setting.

1. Peggy Kern titled her selection "Two Lives Too Many." Why do you think she chose that title? What idea do you think she is trying to convey?

2. For both Megan and Ryan, many people joined in the cyberbullying attacks. Why? What draws people to participate in something so hurtful? What do you think could be done to discourage people from joining in? Explain.

3. After Ryan's death, it was revealed that most of the students in his school knew what was going on but refused to speak up about it. Have you ever been in a position, like Ryan's classmates, when you knew something wrong was happening but were reluctant to tell anyone? What prevented you from talking?

4. Have you encountered behavior in a social networking site or online that bothered you or made you uncomfortable? What happened? What did you do?

TOPICS TO WRITE ABOUT

Below are three writing assignments based on the situations and ideas in Kern's essay. Each invites you to put your thoughts about cyberbullying into writing.

1. **Writing a Script:** Many people react to cyberbullying by either joining in the behavior or ignoring it as if it were a harmless joke. What if, instead, those witnesses responded differently? Write the script for a cyberbullying encounter in a chat room in which a witness decides to take a stand. The following is the format for writing a script:

   Ralph: OMG did you see Sarah in school today? That girl is so fat she needs her own zip code.

   Omar: LOL, she's as big as a house!!!

   Keisha: Both of you leave Sarah alone. She never did nothing to you . . .

   Try to make the conversations as realistic as possible. What exactly would the characters say to each other? What, if anything, could they say to stop their behavior? Try to express, through the characters' words, the kinds of emotions they are feeling.

   Begin your script with a narrator who explains who the characters are, how they are communicating (on Facebook, MySpace, or texting, for example), and how they managed to end up in the online conversation.

   Your script might then be performed in class, with one student as the narrator, another as the bully, and a third as the person who steps in to stop the bully.

2. **Writing a Paragraph:** Many peers of Megan and Ryan knew of the cyberbullying they faced. Yet they didn't intervene. How do you feel about their decision? Was it cruel? Cowardly? Understandable? Justified? Write a paragraph in which you explain what you think of those who witnessed what was happening. Give at least three reasons to support your opinion.

3. **Writing an Essay:** From reading this essay, and from your own experiences, what advice would you give others to protect themselves from cyberbullying? Imagine you are writing for a child or younger sibling. Write an essay that presents the three (or more) main suggestions you think young people should know. You may begin your essay with this thesis statement: "There are three keys to avoid cyberbullying." In your essay, explain each of the three points you present. Make sure to include examples or specific details about each point so your readers understand exactly what you mean. Feel free to include any real examples from your life experience to support your points.

PART 3:
WHAT TO DO ABOUT BULLYING

Just because bullying is common does not mean you must accept it. There are steps you can take to reduce bullying. As key members of a school community, you and your peers have the most to gain from reducing this hurtful behavior. You also share the biggest responsibility for what happens. While you alone can't change the entire climate of your school, you can change how *you* respond.

Part 3 of this book lists practical steps you can take to reduce bullying in your school. These steps are divided into four groups. The first focuses on what you can do if you are targeted by bullies; the second includes strategies for bystanders; the third gives suggestions for those accused of bullying, and the last includes steps to take when dealing with cyberbullying.

What You Can Do When You Are Being Bullied

Anyone who has been the target of a bully knows how lonely and difficult it can be. But people singled out by bullies are not powerless. If a bully's attention is aimed at you, there are actions you can take to prevent or diminish the attack. Some of these strategies are quiet and involve developing a healthy and realistic perspective, a kind of mental shield. Others are more direct and involve responding to your attacker. Not all of the steps described below will work in every situation. However, with patience and practice, you can use these suggestions to help you the next time a bully crosses your path.

1 **Remember that bullying is the problem—not you.** If you are currently dealing with a bully, don't be ashamed or embarrassed. There's nothing "wrong" with you that makes you deserve such treatment. Even if others target you for being "different" for whatever reason, they do NOT have the right to insult or mistreat you. All of us deserve civility. As human beings, we have a right to be free from threats, cruelty, and violence. Those who attack people for their differences—whether it be based on appearance, sexual preference, disability, race, or something else—have engaged in unacceptable behavior. They have failed to be civil. They are the source of the problem, not you.

Understand, too, that it is completely normal to feel anger, sadness, fear, and depression because of bullying. You are not "weak" or "soft" or "a sissy" because you have such feelings. Anyone who says otherwise simply doesn't know how tough it is to face such treatment. Each day tens of thousands of your peers in schools throughout the country feel the exact same emotions when faced with bullying. You are not alone.

2 **Remember that bullying is not permanent.** The awful days will pass. During school, especially in grades 6 through 10, bullying can be so constant that you may feel your life will always be filled with peers who exist just to humiliate you. This is not true. In the adult world, such behavior is unacceptable and even illegal. In the future, you will be free from the hurtful teasing and insults of today. When you are an adult, you will look back, and the bully and his or her friends will be long gone. The torment you endure now will be over. You may even find yourself working in a position where you'll be able to help protect kids from bullies. Keep this in mind at all times, especially when you're sad or hurt. There is a better future waiting for you.

3 **Understand several facts about bullies.** First, bullies are often (but not always) lonely and insecure people. When they pick on you, they stop others from picking on them. They feel safer, stronger, and in control when they bully—feelings that might be missing in other parts of their lives.

A second fact about bullies is that they often want desperately to be accepted by "the crowd." For this reason, they sometimes intensify their attacks when they have audiences around them. But the truth is that the people in the crowd often care little for the bully. Instead, they "go along" with things because they, too, are afraid. In other words, many who join the bully in teasing you are not necessarily your enemies. Some are simply acting mean so the bully does not turn against them. Many students are guilty of such "fake" behavior.

A final fact about bullies is that the high status they may enjoy in school does not last. Physical, verbal, or social bullying is not accepted in the adult world. Those who rely on it to deal with their peers risk facing lifelong difficulties in their jobs, their communities, and their personal relationships. In one study, one-third of male bullies between sixth and ninth grades ended up with criminal convictions by age 24. In another study, bullies were shown to be five times more likely than their non-bullying peers to have criminal records by age 30. While not every bully becomes a criminal, there is plenty of evidence that bullying, instead of making a person socially successful, can lead to serious problems and unhappiness.

4 **If at all possible, tell someone else about your experience.** Embarrassment, shame, and fear cause many who are bullied to hide their experiences from others. This decision only increases the isolation and pain of bullying, and it can lead to depression.

Talking to others eases these negative feelings and allows you to express the anger and hurt building up inside. If you are being bullied, find someone you can trust and tell him or her what you are facing. If you have no one nearby to speak to, consider writing your thoughts in a journal, notebook, or computer. In each case, be careful not to leave your words where your peers or bullies can see them.

While talking and writing are not going to solve your problem, the simple act of expressing your true feelings will allow you to "vent" and help you feel a bit better.

5 **Find safety in numbers.** Bullies often pick on people who are isolated. Students who walk to school alone, sit by themselves in class, or eat alone at lunch are more likely to get harassed. Because such people are outside "the crowd," bullies are freer to pick on them.

So, whenever you can, keep people around you. If a bully attacks you in an isolated hallway, try to use a more crowded hallway next time. If you normally sit alone at lunchtime, take a risk and join a table where you know someone who seems nice. When on a school bus, sit as close to the driver as you can. Instead of walking alone to school, walk in or very close to a larger crowd of students. Remember, there is often safety in numbers.

6 Tell a school official. Very few people who are targeted by bullies feel comfortable telling school officials what is happening. Some fear that telling a teacher, principal, coach, or guidance counselor will make the bully retaliate with even harsher treatment. Others are simply too ashamed to admit the truth. Many think that telling teachers about bullies is "soft" or cowardly. Finally, some do not wish to be "a snitch." While these reasons are understandable, each is wrong and unhelpful. Here's why:

First of all, when you tell school officials about a bully, you help other students who are in need. Chances are the bully that picks on you also attacks some of your peers. And like you, those other students may think the best way to respond is to keep quiet. As a result, you and many other students may be enduring daily misery simply because you refuse to speak up. If you're not willing to talk to a teacher for yourself, try doing it for your peers. Others will be quietly grateful to you for being brave enough to take a stand. And, most likely, you will feel relieved once you are able to tell a trusted official what has been happening.

A second reason to tell a teacher or counselor about a bully's behavior is that you might protect future students from avoidable suffering; you may even prevent a tragedy. People who endure the harsh treatment of bullies can reach a breaking point, a time when they are so depressed, angry and frustrated that they are ready to hurt themselves or others. If school officials are alerted to what is happening, there is a chance to prevent such moments. Sadly, school shootings and suicides happen each year because people are too scared to speak up. Despite what some say about being a "snitch," alerting a teacher or principal is not an act of cowardice; it is an act of bravery. Your action may save lives. If more students did it, schools would be safer for everyone.

For all the reasons above, it is important, even critical, that you let school officials know when bullies are acting up. Keep in mind that there are many ways to do this. You don't have to do it publicly in the middle of the school day. You may be able to do it privately after school when you can speak with a teacher one-on-one. Or you can write an anonymous letter, send an e-mail message, or place a phone call (or have a trusted adult in your life do this) so that your classmates don't know what you have done. All this may seem extreme, but remember that lives could be at stake.

7 Get active. School sports, clubs, and organizations can be safe havens from bullies. When you join a group activity, you become part of a community that is likely to watch and protect its members. In addition, school activities are places to make friends as well as meet helpful adults, including coaches, mentors, and faculty advisors. For this reason, getting active can be one of the healthiest and safest steps you can take to reduce bullying in your life.

If traditional school sports make you uncomfortable, find something else that better matches your interests. For example, your school might have a volunteer organization, a marching band, a chess team, a choral group, or an outdoor club that appeals to you. No matter what you choose, your involvement will lead you to new people and new experiences. And while the idea of joining a new activity may be stressful at first, most people feel much better about themselves when they become part of a group. Keep in mind, if you join an activity and discover that you do not like it, don't get discouraged. Just try something else. Sooner or later you will discover something that you like.

Note: If your school has no organizations that appeal to you, find out what's available in your community. The YMCA/YWCA, community centers, libraries, and churches/synagogues/mosques often have activities available for young people. Typically, such organizations are eager for new participants. They want you to join them.

8 Use specific responses to deal with the bully. There is no simple way to deal with bullies when they strike. Each bully is different, and what you do in one situation may not work in another. The tips presented below offer a variety of different ways to react when a bully confronts you. Some of them may work with the bullies in your school; others may not.

■ **Laugh along.** Bullies often take pleasure in upsetting the people they attack. If you laugh along with a bully's insults, you actually take away some of his or her power. The next time a bully teases you, you might laugh as if you are part of the joke. Your response suggests to others that teasing doesn't upset you.

■ **Roll with the punch.** In boxing, a punch can be made less damaging if the target moves in the same direction as the hit. The same idea is true for insults. When a bully teases you, agree with what is said. You may even want to add or expand the bully's insult. For example, a bully might pick on you for wearing glasses. You might say, "Yep, I've got four eyes. That's right, my eyes are just like bug eyes. Thanks for pointing that out."

This tactic steals away the bully's power and control. How can he or she insult you if you have already done it? Because the bully has less to gain from targeting you, he or she may skip you in future verbal attacks.

■ **Change the subject.** When a bully hassles you, point out something that distracts his or her negative attention. You might say something like, "Oh no, that teacher is watching us. You better do this later." Or you might simply look at something around you and use it as a question or distraction: "What's that teacher's problem?" Your effort is likely to confuse the bully and buy you time. Combined with other strategies in this list, distraction can be an effective response to a bully's verbal attack.

■ **Learn verbal self defense.** Some verbal bullies—those who are not physically violent—may be discouraged if you defend yourself verbally. This does not mean you should get into a shouting match or scream insults in your school hallway; such behavior will get you in trouble and worsen the situation. Instead, it means developing a response to a bully's verbal attack, one which shows bullies there is nothing to be gained from teasing you.

Keep in mind that bullies typically want to see their targets get emotional. For this reason, it is important that you stay calm and deny the bully the pleasure of upsetting you. Having a quick comeback is one way to show a verbal bully you are not an easy target. Below are some responses that can ward off a verbal bully's attack.

- ☐ **Give the bully permission to tease you.** This gives *you* control and power in the situation, not the bully. *Example:* "Go ahead, Lisa. Say what you want. It's not gonna bother me."

- ☐ **Act as if you don't care.** This denies bullies the satisfaction of making you upset. Speak calmly to show you're in control. *Example:* "Whatever, Lisa."

- ☐ **Act as if you have other things to worry about.** This takes away the bully's control and puts you in charge while also deflecting the attack. Example: "I'm sorry, Lisa, but I don't have time for this. I need to be home now."

- ☐ **Address the bully's attack directly.** Done with respect and eye contact, this gesture puts you on equal footing with him or her. It also shows your expectation of civility. It may also win you respect among bystanders. Example: "C'mon, Lisa. Let's just stop this. We both have better things to do."

- ☐ **Reject the bully's insults.** This assertive step declares your power and dignity to everyone that hears you. Example: "You have no right to talk to me that way. I have nothing to say to you, Lisa. I'm done."

In each case, the best approach after these suggestions is to walk away and remove yourself from the bullying situation. In time, the bully may decide you are not an easy verbal target and move on.

A Warning About Fighting

Many adults—including some parents—think that the best way to deal with bullies is to stand up and fight them. To be fair, it is true that fighting sometimes works at least temporarily to discourage bullies. However, physical violence is a harmful and unsafe strategy, one that often leads to even more serious problems. For this reason, fighting is an unwise way to deal with a bully. Anyone who tells you otherwise is not being realistic.

First off, most schools have strict "zero-tolerance" policies for fighting. This means that you will be punished for fighting— even if you were provoked or trying to defend yourself from a bully. The punishment may include a suspension or possibly an expulsion from your school, leading you to even bigger troubles.

Second, fights can easily escalate and may not be limited to fists. Knives and guns are far too easy for young people to obtain. If you get into a fight with a bully, it may be impossible for you to know if weapons are present until it is too late. And even if a bully does not have a weapon today, what is to stop him or her from bringing one tomorrow? Each day young people are shot and killed in retaliation for fights that happen in or near school. While there are many reasons fighting is unacceptable, this is the most important.

So if it is at all possible, avoid fighting. Your life is too precious to risk for something that will be just a bad memory in a few years.

ACTIVITY

Your teacher may have you answer the following questions individually or may have you discuss the questions in a small group with other students. In either case, a whole class discussion might follow.

What three steps on pages 44–51 for dealing with bullies are the best ones to use at your school?

_____

_____

_____

_____

_____

_____

_____

_____

Are there other steps you would suggest to deal with bullying? Explain.

_____

_____

_____

_____

_____

_____

_____

_____

What You Can Do If You Witness Bullying

A major reason why bullying is so common is that few witnesses ever stand up against it. Instead, most people who see bullying "laugh along," an act which actually contributes to the problems caused by bullies.

The steps below describe a different, more productive course of action for those who witness bullying. The simplest actions you can take are presented first. More difficult—and braver—suggestions follow. Of course, not every suggestion works for a given situation. Sometimes only one or two options will be possible. What is important is that taking any step, even a small one, is better than doing nothing.

1 Refuse to join in. Bullies are almost always accompanied by followers who join in their hurtful behavior. Often these people are "going along" with things because they are afraid of the bully. Yet this decision only encourages the bully to continue tormenting people.

Here is what you can do instead: Rather than laughing along or teasing the bully's target, just stay quiet. If you refuse to participate, the bully has less encouragement to continue his or her behavior. Also, your decision to "stay out of it" means that one less person—you—is hurting the bully's target.

2 Walk away when bullies are acting up. Most people gather quickly to watch bullying take place. Bullies thrive on this attention, and their targets suffer more because of it. By removing yourself from the mob of onlookers, you reduce the amount of attention the bully is getting. Also, the act of walking away can send a quiet message that you don't approve of what is happening.

3 Distract the bully. Bullies, like everyone else, can be distracted. Sometimes changing the subject, telling an unrelated story or joke, or just encouraging the bully to do something else ("Let's go outside / get back to class / head home / get something to eat") can prevent a hurtful incident from happening. This is not a permanent solution, but it may be enough to spare one of your classmates from another moment of torment.

4 **Report any bullying you see.** Many students witness bullying but refuse to tell adults because they don't want to "rat out" someone. But if you know someone is being hassled or about to do something harmful to another person (or him/herself), alert a trusted teacher or school official to the problem.

Here's one way to proceed: Instead of "telling on" the bully, you might express concern for the person who is being targeted. You might say, "I'm worried about Eric because people keep teasing him." If you are afraid of what others might say, you could report what you know anonymously either by writing an unsigned letter or calling the principal but not leaving your name. The important thing is that school officials are made aware of the problem so something can be done about it.

5 **Speak out.** This step is a bit more difficult and takes courage. If possible, get a friend or two to join you. When you see bullying taking place, speak out against it. Simple phrases like "Leave her alone" or "Stop picking on him" can really undermine the control a bully has. If you and other people protest, the bully will become uncomfortable and is likely to stop the hurtful behavior. Doing so may result in people turning on him or her, and that's the last thing a bully wants to happen.

6 **Stand up.** This is a brave and highly effective way to deal with bullies. When someone is being teased or intimidated, walk over and stand with that person. Or simply invite him or her to join your group of friends. Your action will send a message that the target is not alone—and that bullying behavior will not be tolerated. If you manage to gather several people, the bully will probably go away. Keep in mind that your behavior is not intended to insult or harm the bully. Instead, it is meant to prevent or stop another attack.

7 **Work with others to reduce bullying.** Even schools that have serious problems with bullies can be changed into much safer and friendlier places. To make this happen, you and your classmates must work with other students and teachers to increase the strength of your school's community.

One way to begin is to set up a meeting in which students and teachers talk openly about bullying. Speak to your principal, teacher, or counselor about reserving a time to discuss concerns about the problem of bullying in your school.

At the meeting, try to come up with specific actions which can be taken to reduce bullying. Maybe you and your peers can discuss ways to resolve conflicts and to better treat isolated or new students. Or perhaps you know of a place in or near the school that is unsafe and could use better security. Prepare specific suggestions for teachers and administrators on how they can support what you're trying to do. Sometimes simply increasing the amount of adult supervision in the cafeteria and in bathrooms is enough to significantly reduce bullying in school. Whatever actions you suggest will be more effective if everyone—students, teachers, and principals—comes together to support them.

Distributing copies of this booklet to parents and other members of the school community is another way to reduce bullying in your school. Once bullies sense that many eyes are on them—and that their behavior is being observed—they will be less likely to hurt others.

Your teacher may have you answer the following questions individually or may have you discuss the questions in a small group with other students. In either case, a whole class discussion might follow.

Which three steps on pages 53-55 for witnesses of bullying are the best ones to use at your school?

_____

_____

_____

_____

_____

_____

_____

_____

Are there other steps you would suggest for witnesses of bullying to help reduce this problem? Explain.

_____

_____

_____

_____

_____

_____

_____

_____

What You Can Do If You or Someone Else Thinks You're a Bully

Being a bully isn't easy. It means you have to behave in ways that make others dislike you. You must be constantly on the lookout to "prove yourself" so no one thinks you are weak or unpopular. And you must do things—such as threaten, tease, and hurt others—that are wrong, punishable, dangerous, and even illegal. But more than anything, bullying puts you on an isolating and lonely path that often leads to trouble and sadness.

When you are a bully, it is almost impossible to have true friends. First of all, your targets are likely to hate and resent you because of how you treat them. Your peers may act nice, but secretly many of them are fearful and distrustful of you. They may conclude that you are just a mean person. In time, if you mistreat people long enough, they will start to avoid you. You may wind up with a few "fake" friends and many quiet enemies.

As you read this section, remember that you don't have to act tough or hurt others to get respect, laughs, or friends. You can be strong without hurting people; you can be popular without making someone else feel bad. The steps below will show you how.

1 **Learn to watch your behavior.** Many students who tease and hassle others do not fully realize that their actions are hurtful. Sometimes they think they are "just kidding around" and that others take them too seriously. If you think you might be a bully, or if others—peers, teachers, or parents—accuse you of bullying, you may fall into this category.

Starting today, pay close attention to your behavior. Are you saying or doing things that may be hurtful to others? Does your "playing around" or "joking" seem to upset your peers? What could you do instead? Your effort to become aware and sensitive to what you are doing may help you make positive changes.

2 **Remain silent or walk away.** To a bully, a shy student sitting alone in the cafeteria or on the school bus may look like an easy target for a mean joke or rude comment. If other students are nearby, the bullying impulse may be even stronger. Bullies crave attention and respect, and they find the lure of a crowd's laughter hard to resist.

If you feel tempted to tease or hassle someone, fight the impulse. Instead of opening your mouth, simply turn and walk away. No one will think you are weak or "soft" if you do this. Yet you will prevent yourself from saying or doing something you might regret. In addition, you will have just saved someone from enduring a painful or embarrassing experience.

3 **Talk to a trusted adult.** If you find yourself constantly teasing or hurting others, try talking to someone about it. Perhaps you have a family member, coach, neighbor, or community leader whom you trust. Try telling one of these adults what's on your mind. While at first it might seem strange to talk to someone, you may be surprised at how relieved you feel knowing that someone else listens to and understands you. You may also discover what drives you to treat your peers so harshly. Perhaps there are triggers you can avoid.

Taking this step is not easy. It requires bravery and patience as you search for a person you trust. But when you find such a person and begin speaking openly with him or her, you're almost sure to feel better about yourself and life in general.

4 **Seek other help.** Some people who hurt others need help that parents and friends cannot provide. If you feel that you cannot control your behavior or you simply want help as you try to change, reach out to a professional, such as a teacher, a guidance counselor, or a school psychologist.

Seeking help is a big decision, one which can seem incredibly frightening. But understand that many folks—including athletes, celebrities, and everyday people—quietly get professional assistance each day. To reach the point where you would ever think about doing this is an important step, and it deserves praise.

and respect. Consider this fact: many adults know they have serious emotional problems but are too scared to do anything about them. Instead they endure problems in silence for years, causing pain to their families because they refuse to get help. It doesn't have to be this way for you.

Start by scheduling time during lunch or after school to talk to a teacher or advisor you like. Explain your situation by saying something like, "Mrs. Herndon, I keep trying to leave Gerald alone. But I can't help it. I feel really bad each time I tease him, but sometimes I can't stop. I'm telling you because I'm tired of acting this way, and I want to change."

The adult you speak with may want to contact your parents or guardians, but if there are problems at home that might be worsened by a phone call, be sure to say so. School officials do not wish to make your life more difficult. If they understand what is going on, they're likely to do whatever is in their power to help you.

5 Get active. Many students who tease and torment others do so because they have negative feelings about themselves. When, for example, they point out someone's flaws, they distract others from noticing theirs. Picking on others also gives them short-lived feelings of respect, power, and self-esteem. But these feelings, which come from negative behaviors, don't last and almost always lead to serious trouble. Fortunately, there are positive ways to gain true and lasting self-esteem.

Activities—sports, clubs, hobbies, volunteer work, and jobs—are great ways to gain experiences and skills that will make you feel better about yourself without having to harm others. Schools often have a range of activities open to students. Traditional sports teams are the most well-known student organizations, but there are others. The school newspaper, drama/theater clubs, chorus, or marching band are some other popular ways to get involved. Many schools also offer clubs based on hobbies, such as chess, computers, or dancing. Some schools feature organizations that focus on academic topics or languages and cultures. Your school, for example, might have a History or Science Club, a Spanish or French Club, or an Asian students' organization. Why not join one that interests you?

If nothing at your school appeals to you, look for an activity outside of school. Community organizations, such as the YMCA/YWCA or PAL (among others), offer a variety of activities for young people, ranging from martial arts lessons to community service projects. If you like the idea of doing "real" work, consider volunteering at a local library, assisting at a neighborhood food bank or animal shelter, or helping to keep a nearby park clean. Many community organizations need and want young people to help them. Getting involved has the potential not only to make you feel better about yourself; it can also be fun. And there's always the chance you might find new friends or get to know helpful adults while you're doing your activity.

Another option is to get a job after school. In addition to making money, you'll meet people, gain valuable skills, and build self-esteem. Of course, you have to be old enough (at least 14 in many states), and you should have the support of your parent or guardian. Once you begin working, you'll discover how important it is to give and get respect from those around you. In a professional setting—a restaurant, movie theater, supermarket or mall for example—you'll find that teamwork and friendliness are rewarded. The negative behaviors of school bullies—cruelty intimidation, and rudeness—are not tolerated. In "real-world" situations, the nicer and friendlier you are, the more respect and success you will have.

All the activities above—sports, clubs, volunteer work, and jobs—promise to give you meaningful experiences that will make you stronger, wiser, and more confident. You'll come to realize that you don't need to be mean or hurtful to gain respect from others. And you'll see that you don't need the pain of vulnerable people or the laughter of the crowd to make you feel good about yourself. By being brave enough to join an activity and patient enough to give it a chance, you'll discover that there is a better world out there for you, a world where bullying makes no sense

6 **Apologize.** One of the bravest and most difficult actions for a bully to take is to apologize for doing something wrong. If you say "I'm sorry," or "I was wrong to treat you that way" to a person you have bullied, you're taking a powerful step. Your words, whether they are accepted or not, tell everyone that you know what you did was wrong and that you want to avoid such behavior in the future. An apology in private is strong all by itself, and an apology in public can be even more powerful. In either case, a sincere apology is a sign of adulthood, maturity, and strength. If you mean your words, you will earn respect for having the courage to say them.

7 **Become an anti-bully.** Each day thousands of bullies move through schools hurting and wounding their peers. An anti-bully is a person who, instead of practicing cruelty each day, practices kindness. He or she looks for the shy, isolated students in school and makes sure they are treated fairly. When a bully starts mistreating someone, an anti-bully will step in, either by verbally discouraging the bully or by standing with the target so he or she is not alone. Your behavior may frustrate the bully—and he or she may tease or mock you for it. However, your actions will also win gratitude and respect, especially from the many people who endure bullies in your school.

By becoming an anti-bully, you gain popularity and status without hurting anyone. You also become a model for other students to follow, and you make your school a safer place for everyone. Most importantly, you behave in ways guaranteed to make you feel better about yourself. It is a difficult road, but in the long run, it is far more rewarding than being a bully.

What You Can Do About Cyberbullying

Will you send a text message or visit a social networking site today? If you are like millions of American teens, the answer is yes. In recent years, technology has transformed the way people—especially young people—communicate. It has changed bullying, too.

Unheard of a decade or so ago, cyberbullying has grown to be a major menace in middle and high schools, affecting more than one-third of students today. It is fueled by the same forces that drive other forms of bullying, and it includes the same participants: bullies, targets, and bystanders. In some ways, however, cyberbullying is more hurtful than the meanest face-to-face insults. Here's why:

The Internet is always on. Cyberbullies can harass whenever they want. Students who would normally relax once they get home from school now find themselves the targets of hostile texts, instant messages, chat rooms, or "pages" at all hours of the day. Besides being constant, cyberbullying tends to involve a large audience. In school, an insult may circulate among a clique of students over the course of a day; online it can spread to hundreds in a matter of seconds. Complete strangers can see and add to the online torment, and it may take days or longer before offensive material gets removed. This can be crushing, especially to someone who endures other forms of bullying each day.

Another reason cyberbullying is so painful is that it is difficult to know who is doing it. On the Internet, bullies can hide their identities to avoid getting in trouble. Some create false profiles (or use a different person's account) to launch their attacks. A few go further and pretend to be friends with their targets, getting them to reveal private and often embarrassing information. Later, these false online "friends" share this information publicly, an act of betrayal that humiliates those who are targeted.

The Internet itself seems to encourage bullying. Unlike at school, there are no officials nearby to protect students online. Those who bully know this and feel freer to attack. Others not bold enough to bully in-person may do it over the Internet where their identity is concealed. Hidden anonymously behind a keyboard, they can hurl ugly words without ever being held responsible.

The impact of these attacks can be tragic. Young people, desperate and depressed as a result of cyberbullying, have taken their own lives in communities across the United States. For them and the countless others enduring cyberbullying, it is critical that you understand the dangers of this behavior and try to stop it.

Below is a list of steps you can take to combat cyberbullying. It is divided into three parts. The first includes precautions to reduce your exposure to this problem. The second presents practical steps if you are the target of cyberbullying. The third presents steps to follow if you encounter or witness cyberbullying.

1. What you can do to prevent cyberbullying

■ **Know your "friends."** When you're using a social networking site, it's tempting to "friend" as many people as possible. Some users allow hundreds—even thousands—of people to view their online profile. This may seem impressive. After all, the more "friends" you have, the more popular you are, right? Wrong. In reality, few people know hundreds of individuals well enough to call them friends. Would you let a stranger view photos of you, read your inner thoughts, and know where you go to school? When you "friend" someone you don't know, that's what you've done. Be smart online. Only "friend" people you know and trust in real life.

■ **Protect your accounts.** Never share log-in information or passwords for your electronic accounts. This includes e-mail, instant message services, social networking sites, and online video games. In the wrong hands, these details can be used to access your private conversations, steal your identity, commit crimes, and cause great harm. If you suspect that someone other than a trusted parent or guardian knows your password, change it immediately. If necessary, contact the service provider to suspend your stolen account.

- **Use privacy settings.** Most social networking sites allow you to control what others can see of your profile. Research your settings and configure them so that only people who are your friends can view your profile. This will prevent strangers or potential bullies from seeing what you want only your friends to see. In addition, these settings can stop others from posting on your page.

- **Keep private information private.** Avoid posting revealing personal information, photographs, inner thoughts, or intimate details about your home life or loved ones on the Internet. Despite privacy settings, it is possible that some of what you put online will be seen by people who are not your friends. And once this material gets on the Internet, it can exist there for a long time—even after you delete it from your local computer. To protect yourself, imagine that everything you put online will be seen by your worst enemy. If what you are about to post is something you wouldn't want your enemy to read, don't put it on the Internet.

2. What you can do if you are the target of cyberbullying

- **Keep perspective.** Cyberbullying attacks can be agonizing. You may feel desperate, alone, and cornered. It may seem that the attacks are unstoppable and neverending. This is not true. As bad as you feel, know that this day will pass. The cruelty you're enduring now will not always be with you. A future awaits you where you'll be free of this behavior. Hold on to this idea when you're feeling sad and overwhelmed. One day you will look back on the events of today, and they will be a memory. You'll see. Knowing the future will be bully-free, you can focus on taking steps to to reduce the problem right now. As you'll see below, you have some choices.

- **Don't respond online.** Bullies want to upset you. If you respond online to an attack, you show the bully that he or she has succeeded. In addition, you make yourself a bigger target for future attacks from the bully or others who might want to join in. By refusing to respond online, you deny the bully the satisfaction of knowing he or she upset you. In time, the bully may simply get bored and stop targeting you.

■ **Block the bully's attacks.** Cell phones can be set to block the numbers of people you don't wish to reach you. E-mail and instant message services can block senders. Facebook and other social networking services allow you to block people from corresponding with you. Set each device and account to block those people you want to avoid. While this won't stop them from talking about you, it will prevent their threats or insults from reaching your account or being posted to your profile.

■ **Change your accounts.** Cyberbullies need to be able to find you to attack you. Just as bullies can mask their identity, so can you. For example, if someone sends you threatening texts, you can request to get a new number from your cell phone provider. Most will do this for free, especially if you explain the reason. Once your number is switched, the bully won't know your new number and will be unable to text you.

Similarly, you can change your screen name or delete a social networking profile if it is being targeted. You may temporarily lose connections to your old friends, but you can reestablish them easily enough by creating a new account. Just be careful. If you tell others about your new screen name, profile, or phone number, bullies may find out and target you again.

■ **Record the attack.** Unlike face-to-face bullying, cyberbullying always leaves evidence. If you feel as if you are being attacked, record—do not delete—anything said about you. Save all e-mails, instant messages, texts or links related to the attack. If a chat room or group is targeting you, take a screen shot of the activity. (Most computers have this feature built in. Search "taking screenshots" in Google for directions if you need them). Try to note the date and times of each attack (most programs include this information automatically). The information you record will reveal details about those responsible for the attacks. In addition, it will be valuable if you choose to report the attacks later on.

- **Talk to a trusted adult.** If you're the target of cyberbullying, don't endure the attacks in silence. Doing so only leads to depression and isolation. To combat these feelings, talk to adults who care about you. Tell them what you're experiencing. While talking does not stop the problem, it will allow you to vent and help you feel better. If the adult is supportive, show him or her your record of the attacks mentioned above. After talking with the adult, you can decide if you want to take additional steps to deal with the problem.

- **Tell the service provider.** Social networking sites, cell phone companies, and instant message services have policies to protect users from cyberbullying. In Facebook, for example, you can report the user, any messages he's sent, or any pages he's created with the click of a button. Doing so alerts the company that a user is behaving in an abusive and inappropriate way. In time, the account is likely to be closed and the hurtful information taken down. MySpace and other sites have similar functions. You can also report messages to your cell phone provider. Each company's reporting procedures are different, but they all take cyberbullying seriously. If you bring it to their attention, they will do what they can to stop it. In addition, you'll limit the bully's ability to launch electronic attacks at you or anyone else.

- **Report the attack to a school official.** Cyberbullying is a crime. No one has the right to threaten, harass, or intimidate another person online. Laws exist to protect people from this behavior. But for them to work, students need to speak up when cyberbullies strike. By sharing details of the attack with a principal or teacher, you give them what they need to help you.

  At first, it may seem strange and uncomfortable to talk to a school official about a cyberbullying attack. But keep in mind, you are not alone. Many people endure similar attacks but are too frightened to say anything about it. By speaking up, you take a stand for them and for yourself. Your actions will draw much needed attention to this problem so your school can better protect students. Your story will also teach school officials who might not know the technology as well as you do. Future students will benefit from what you do. So while part of you may feel awkward, know that telling authorities is a brave act. You could play a vital role in making your school safer for all students. You deserve praise for coming forward!

■ **Unplug and go offline.** While it may seem extreme, you can always cancel whatever services are receiving attacks. Of course, you'll lose the accounts, but you'll also shut down the bully's access to you. Your gesture can be an act of ultimate defiance. Those who enjoy upsetting you will no longer have you as a target. This may not prevent them from talking about you, but it is the best armor against online attacks. When you have no online accounts, cyberbullying is much less effective against you.

3. What you can do if you witness cyberbullying

■ **Check yourself.** Many people who witness cyberbullying dismiss it as a joke, something not to be taken seriously. It may seem that way when you're reading a post online or laughing along with a group of your friends. However, it is never a joke when other people are being hurt, humiliated, threatened, or harassed. Many have made the mistake of accepting this cruel online behavior as "normal," and lives have been lost as a result. When you witness cyberbullying, understand that you are seeing a serious problem— one that should be stopped. Keep that in mind as you decide on other actions you can take.

■ **Don't participate.** If someone forwards you a text, image, or link that will hurt or embarrass another person, delete it. If you know there is a chat room, page, or posting where someone is attacking a peer, avoid it, and don't share it with others. Remember, bullies enjoy the attention and control they get from their behavior. By spreading harmful material online, you increase the power of the bully's attack and the damage it causes. By removing your own participation, you can help limit the problem.

- **Block the sender and his or her attacks.** This takes just a click or two on most social networking sites or instant message programs, but it will reduce by one—you—the number of people receiving the cyberbully's attack.

- **Tell the sender to stop.** Very few people actually protest cyberbullying when they see it. Like bystanders of other forms of bullying, they observe what's happening but refuse to get involved. While fear motivates some to remain quiet, others do so because they have accepted it as normal behavior. You don't have to accept cyberbullying. Rather than remaining silent, send a text or instant message, or post a comment telling the cyberbully to stop what he or she is doing. Your words, especially if they are posted in a chat room or public forum, will also show others that not everyone approves of what the bully is doing. Keep in mind, you can send your comment anonymously or through a temporary screen name if you fear retaliation. At the very least, your gesture will serve as notice to all those involved that what they are doing is wrong. Perhaps others will follow your lead.

- **Report cyberbullying to the service provider.** Popular social networking sites, online video games, and chat rooms allow users to report cyberbullying. In Facebook, for example, you have the option to "report" comments, pictures, or pages that are "abusive." Doing this is anonymous. The bully will never know who reported him or her. The service provider will then review the account. If the user is found to be cyberbullying, his or her account will suspended. Keep in mind, each company's reporting procedures are different, but they all take cyberbullying seriously, and most have steps in place to report it. If they don't, seek another provider who does.

- **Show support to those being cyberbullied.** Be friendly—in person and online—with those you know who are being bullied. You can also show support online by "friending" the target or posting comments that indicate you stand against the mistreatment you see. Your actions may encourage others to respond similarly

In addition, your friendly gesture may be just what the targeted person needs after being attacked.

■ **Share what you see with school officials.** If you are concerned about a cyberbullying situation in school, record what is happening. Save messages, texts, comments, and even screenshots of the attacks. You can then share this information with a school official. This can be done directly by forwarding the material to a principal or teacher. Or, if you are uncomfortable with that approach, you can print what details you have and hand them in anonymously. This way, the student or students who are being targeted will not be alone in their struggle. In addition, by bringing the problem to the attention of school officials, you make sure that help is directed toward those who need it.

■ **Use the Internet to combat cyberbullying.** The tools used in cyberbullying can also be used to combat it. Talk to a teacher or school official about using a social networking site to create an online group—or even a real school organization—against cyberbullying. Using Facebook, you could create a page for your group, such as Wagner Middle School Against Bullying. Perhaps you can invite friends, parents, and/or teachers to join the group. You and your teacher could host discussions and share ideas about reducing bullying in schools. You might post instructions for students so they know how to report cyberbullying when they see it. You might even link your site or page to other groups with the same purpose. The possibilities are endless! Just be sure to coordinate with an official at your school so you have the right information and support in your group.

This suggestion above is just one idea. You may have others. In each case, you're taking the technology of cyberbullying and putting it to good use. In time, you may create a popular resource to make your school safer.

Perhaps you'll start today!

ACTIVITY

Cyberbullying is a growing problem affecting young people. Has it impacted your school? Answer "yes" or "no" to the questions below about your online experiences. When you're done, compare your responses to those of your peers.

___ 1. Do you use a computer, cell phone, or video game that connects to the Internet?

___ 2. Do you belong to a social networking site?

___ 3. Have you ever seen an online group, web page, Internet video, or poll that targets another person?

___ 4. Have you ever witnessed behavior in an online video game, chat room, or discussion board that you thought was offensive or cruel to another person?

___ 5. Have you ever created a false online profile or hid your name while online?

___ 6. Have you ever sent something from someone else's cell phone, instant message, or social networking account?

___ 7. Have you ever forwarded a private text, instant message, e-mail, or picture without permission from the original sender?

___ 8. Have you ever posted a picture or video online of people without getting their permission?

About your answers: If you answered "yes" to questions 1–2, you're a potential target of cyberbullying. As of 2008, 32% of students were targets of cyberbullying. If you answered "yes" to questions 3–4, you've encountered cyberbullying. If you answered "yes" to questions 5–8, you've engaged in behavior that could contribute to cyberbullying. Be sure to use only your own account and always get permission before forwarding or sharing personal material online.

A Final Thought:
KINDNESS COUNTS

For everyone—bullies, witnesses, and targets—life is too precious for bullying. Each day, people get sick, loved ones die, and catastrophes strike. Sooner or later, bad things will happen to all of us. If life is so hard, why then do we make matters worse by being hard on each other?

Over many centuries, scholars and religious thinkers have considered this question and searched for a healthy principle to guide people in their everyday lives. One clear answer can be found in history. This rule for living, present in all the world's great religions and cultures, can be summed up in two short words:

Be kind.

Each day is your chance to put this simple rule into practice. Anyone can do it, but not everyone does. What about you? By being friendly to another person, by sitting next to someone who is alone, by refusing to laugh at another person when others do, by choosing not to go along with the behavior of a hurtful crowd, you are practicing kindness.

In the course of preparing this booklet, editors at Townsend Press spoke with students at a number of schools. In addition to getting their input about bullying, we asked them for their reaction to the following observation by the Greek philosopher Philo of Alexandria:

Be kind, for everyone you know is fighting a great battle.

Here are some students' responses:

Ryan "Amen. If you haven't fought a battle, you will. Lots of people have hurdles you don't even know about. Everybody is struggling; everyone has issues. Life is not a la-di-da walk through the park. Life isn't easy. We have to care for one another."

Tina "Be a good person, be respectful, because you don't know what people are dealing with. They're having their own problems. You don't want to be judgmental, because you haven't lived that person's life. Being kind is a virtue. And when others see you being kind, they'll treat you so in return. It's infectious."

Aaron "It's like the saying about walking a mile in another person's shoes. It means giving people the benefit of the doubt. The more you learn about them, the more you can understand them. You don't know what happens to people right before you encounter them. You really never know what people are going through."

Jasmin "Sometimes in school there'll be students who don't quite fit in. I've watched and I've seen other students go after them, like wolves in a pack attacking a weak animal. Hello! What's this about? Are we wolves and is school just survival of the fittest? If a kid doesn't quite fit in, that kid may have problems we're lucky enough not to have. We need to be kind."

Almost without fail, we heard students say that kindness really does count. We are all different in so many ways, but what we all share is a common humanity. Being kind to one another is a way to recognize that our shared humanity is more important than the individual differences between us.

It may help to think of kindness as a muscle. Kindness has to be practiced to become effective and strong and natural. Practicing this human skill can make you a better, happier person. Kindness is the antidote to bullying, which thrives when people are afraid to be kind. Your next act of kindness may be enough to lessen another person's pain or give someone hope. If others follow your lead, you can change your classroom, your school, your neighborhood, and even the world.

The choice is yours.

A STEP TO TAKE NOW: If you are ready to stand against bullying, read the **Pledge to Stop Bullying** on the next page. If you agree with what you read there and are truly ready to reject bullying, sign your name on the pledge. Your signature will be a declaration of your brave choice to reject bullying.

PLEDGE TO STOP BULLYING

This contract will be a record of your commitment to reduce bullying in your school. Read each item carefully. Then choose whether you want to sign this pledge. If you decide that you want to help stop bullying, print your name on the line below, and then sign the bottom of the sheet in the space provided. By doing so, you are making a promise to your peers and to your school community. We congratulate you for your brave and important decision!

I, _____, wish to reduce bullying in my school. I agree to:
    (Print your name here)

1. Do my best to treat ALL my peers with respect and dignity in person AND online.

2. Not isolate, threaten, or harm my peers, or hurtfully tease, exclude, insult, or mock them.

3. Try to prevent or discourage my peers from humiliating, threatening, isolating, or harming others.

4. Try to assist any student who is being mistreated, for the simple reason that it is wrong to be unkind to another human being.

5. If I am comfortable doing so, inform my parent/guardian, teacher, or school administrator when I learn about or see hurtful behavior.

_____   _____
Your Signature   *Today's Date*